44

Mark Snyder

44

Also by Mark Snyder:

Books:

Epitaph: A Conceptual Elegy

Come As You Are

Vadatu

Music:

Necessary Evil

Requiem

"The sonnet... it's a stupid form."

Bernadette Mayer,
Kelly Writers House
Philadelphia, PA
10/21/2014

https://www.youtube.com/watch?v=ZC1ZngRJRAk

44

Mark Snyder

RADICAL TOTALITY

2015

First Printing: 2015

ISBN-13: 978-0692408315 (Radical Totality)
ISBN-10: 0692408312

Radical Totality
764 Seven Lakes North
West End, NC 27376

radicaltotality@gmail.com

To the one whose high moral and ethical standard
inspired me to live the writer's dream:

to quit my job and write this book.

A mission driven comprehensive first
review- you've visited this place three times.
If you are served by feedback contact, sign
returning to the lighthouse reimbursed.
Are you the business owner? What we do
to understand relentless fortune space,
a navigational aid distinctively marked
for daytime visibility, I used
solutions that continue to confound
and leverage. Your network understands
the lighthouse built specifically where it stands.
The rising tide began to see the sound,
the Intracoastal Waterway forecast tide,
theology's symbolic suicide.

The free encyclopedia displays

the meaning of success empowering books

so now he's back again to take a look-

a practice process, set of tools, a way,

a path to healing inspiration, act

or process of becoming healthy needs

to reinstall and even restore your speed,

reset your password, verify your stack.

You've lost importance to help their bodies heal.

I can't return to former victims's fates

abroad. Ebola in the United States

is getting snuffed with remarkable zeal.

Disaster backup evidence is clear

and growing by the day despite the fear.

In economics, often action free
provides desire to perform the work
performed with innovation gone berzerk
achieving enterprise accountancy,
objective analytic tracking codes,
a door tag number, or selective fish
and wildlife cleaning up a damaged wish
for refuge. Health insurance plans implode.
Find answers to your conservation works
and benchmark questions management reserved
for consequences that you now deserve
exclusively for Congress members' perks,
improving access, gateway sutures- these
samsara wheelies bringing on disease.

The latest fear requires the knowledge base

of existential reminiscent play

of walking on the moon, a touch of gray

in New York City's underbelly space

perfecting arts and motivation hooks.

Can you infect the world with such a plague?

The evidence support is rather vague

for quantum cascade lasers writing books.

Abbreviated meaning novel genes,

technology, and inspiration fail

to partner with your open source junk mail,

polluting peace with obsolete machines,

inflicting madness epitaxic need

while global offers will update your feed.

Is that a fact? Is this a date? Is there
a coming slaughter, sixty-three percent:
certain thousands will be murdered here,
and if it does, the city, crammed abduction
streaming refuge instant English tools
whose line the echo morning built-in cloud-
connected marriage culture searching
sixty-three percent. I feel she's there.
This wife does not accept atomic time.
My dying innovation killing love,
the doctrine changes dated content tools
where European comet-chasing days
from launch in classic culture fool
the hunger mission outcomes. Get involved
with rolling back the economic sound.

Increasing rapid special focus sends
a kiss-degenerate differential case
from seventh century Anglo-Saxon ends,
and hoverboards explode subversive rates-
the sort of opportunity in place-
directed energetic beams, neutrino mass-
A Prairie Home Companion special pays
to question history's favorite secret work
assaulted by a hepatitis way.
Designed production, scientific- thanks
for your support! We turn to you to make
collect interrogation cheap-shot cranks-
a singing comet plasma consort song
designed to be a fundamental Sun.

Pronunciation word game rescue guides
the action propagation sending faith
and technical assistance or the like.
Addicted homeless men and women faced
a greater conflict global market. Why?
Electric Hindu, Muslim, Buddhist hearts
demanding high performance on the fly,
hard earned reputation who we are,
consortium motorcycle protocols
and guidelines that ensure inclusive peace
to foster welfare seekers' wounded calls
encouraging atonement refugees
with scientific data overview perspective live
perspective of our practice rendezvous.

A hot shot triumph image search
related to a synonym premiere-
the racing edge demanding piled up words
along a current-motivated fear.
Compulsive multilingual networks hunt
the passionate Big Data window test.
Obsessive snowdrift practice in Detroit-
Camaro, Chevrolet solutions lost
professional accountability.
The principal conditioning special teams
discovery supporting MIT
to form ascetic wealth societies.
We offer sincere thanks for your demand.
Perspective isn't oscillator damped.

Complete including all or nearly all
elements or damage to the field
of understanding time, archaic scrawl
pronunciations, authoritative world
selective leading cancer center care.
The archive network mirrored concept, caught
while damaged city planning needs repair,
an accident regardless who's at fault.
The Joint Commission Institute of Faith
(religious data-driven wizard monks)
oversees the language database
in close accord with adolescent punks
beginning systematic open access plans
providing local supervisor scams.

Overt inventive television forced

eclectic crazy sentence doodling by

experimental interests, cancelled and divorced.

The paranormal speakers stay in touch with why

we'll need to work together instantly.

We don't have room for questions on the fly.

The Old Republic protects activity

that meets the standards outlined on this page.

Find answers to your complex problems here.

Improving published Census Bureau guides,

sampling populations every year,

you've found the resource for all suicides-

a range of craft beers for the greater good

taking corporations cyclists would.

Subsistence disambiguation found

express participation specialty

pronunciation vanguards on the ground.

They don't define themselves as free.

The Rorschach hook up neighborhoods too fast

for chiropractic variant support

identified by questionnaires broadcast

designed to help third parties teleport

our vagrant calling military brats

and dentist-purchased symptom error codes

while anthem value options Democrats

utilizing handbook comedones

approved idea availability

instantiated processing quickly.

This type of book expressing mental states

is governed by relationship of words,

persuaded by the Old English cognates

that Shakespeare died of cancer, 23rd

of April 1616, could also be

tuberculosis maybe, or the plague-

the scourge of London, death with certainty.

The house was made of bricks, but rather vague

prestigious institutions leading home

originating customs in the South:

the Library of Congress velodrome,

or punching mighty heroes in the mouth.

You are so brainwashed thinking of the facts

indicating literary acts.

Their courage and tenacity transformed
a sparsely populated wilderness
into a landscape some would try to harm
with racist e-mails leaked with bitterness.
Considerations lawyers try to fine
are grounded in belief economies-
That's just good teaching! Relevant or blind,
a television film academy
working from within for human rights
selected service intellectually.
Designs are based on principles of light
and polytechnic cult film specialties-
proficient previous intervention signs
repulsive memories friendship undermines.

Detecting signals, unresponsive light-
unstable, damaged, injured influence-
distressed, endangered, fragile line of sight
kept secret to avoid coincident
passing information research free.
Do you prefer chaotic dermatomes
to environments pertaining to the key
of searching knowledge outside Google Chrome?
Responsive multipurpose plural nouns
make better boyfriends into macho pigs
easily annoyed by feeling down
and overwhelmed by Aristotle's digs.
A classifying hypercolor mark-
thermochromic people in the dark.

Residential treatment movie star-

A charismatic crazy hothead act

transforms a life when she becomes bizarre.

The ex-offender aspects using rap

on policy, the country's dying young

from cannabis-induced laryngospasm

affecting how we think, feel and mourn-

we cope with life determined by the chasm

busily engaged, homogenized,

resisting reason, disadvantaged, free,

confronting schizophrenic suicide,

chaotic patchworks of community-

a third of those who need it wondering why

languishing in misery and time.

Energizing metabolic news-

efficiency of living source by law.

Remember eating arsenic for abuse?

Smoking killed my father, cancer clawed

breaking news and pulmonary trials.

You will love each other, peer-reviewed

non-profit change, electric mordent child,

mind and body sharp with headline news.

Tons of useful stuff in magazines-

hydraulic fracking crowdsourced expert picks

and influenza virus smartphone genes

with alcoholic zebra finches sick.

Understand engagement equity

through Heathrow taking charge of your well being.

Besides improving atmospheric works
the oceanic airways start at home
or likewise trademark patent office quirks
with friendly navigation packing foam.
The Fish and Wildlife Service habitats
include the former border income tax
detecting homeless foreign acrobats,
a home of cyanide-laced happiness.
The hemispheres enjoy live galleries
from writing second books on crooks or liars
adorning bodies accidentally
killed by 2-year-olds in household fires.
The winter solstice weather wasting time-
defiant comics pearl resilient crime.

A kind of matter, a stimulating style,
narcotic solid present subject themes-
ghostly figures, knocking sound reviled
essential parts of something from a dream.
Significant importance of the form
underlying shadow baking tools
occupying space material storms-
a kind of constitution meant for fools.
Corruption only doing what is best
for the payment gateway signifying need.
Existing samples facing screening tests-
results are published systematically.
New Jersey's right to know: we take on faith
the evidence of things not seen to date.

Name calling, put downs, yelling harshly, all
improper treatment- unfairly, insultingly,
harshly broken bones with alcohol.
There's no excuse for child pornography
or not reporting subtle signs or claims,
the moral panic trauma prevalence
an exception to the OxyContin games
reflexively shouted epidemic rants.
Don't do it alone. We're here to help. Just call
a widespread war against our children's lives.
We have the power to stop authority's pall
of feeling loved, respected, safe and free
to be yourself, different, now aware,
empowered psychoactive wear and tear.

Expertise has just unveiled research
to streaming rumor sites of child support
domains of thumbtack plans for the next big church-
They're wrong. Abandoned code enforcement tort
and integrated backgrounds interface
by injection applications organized
with angular momentum built on faith,
a cost-effective business enterprise.
Look up a zip code, tax enforcement forms,
headquartered gateway tracking shipping freight
efficiency, integrity reformed
persistent urgent question figure eights:
The monarch butterfly must cover ground
proactively approaching ultrasound.

Terrorist attacks this afternoon-
sadly, not authoritative news;
a scathing message responding to cartoons.
Authorities believe they're not Hindus.
Between an endless war on rigid truth,
adherent outrage culture magazines
directed pagan brainwashed voting booths.
In Dammartin-en-Goele they're on the scene
trying to negotiate the terms-
surrender, martyrdom- mujahideen
walking dead alongside French sauternes
northeast of Paris, broken windows spleen
insisting on a hostage-taking fight
defending freedom of expression's right.

Seamless navigation tracking space
related seconds officially been raised.
The touch screen heads-up item will display
improvement opportunities appraised
and has been named a place to run away.
A rising tide is brewing classic ale.
Emergency preparedness marks the day
of difficulty. Patchwork systems fail.
Incarceration, ceasefire, airstrike truce
of hunger strikes, force-feeding manhunt teams.
The state police have said they'll introduce
new comprehensive cleaning product streams.
Abandoned, blighted Fresno properties
stand out against the background circus frieze.

The transfer fixture moments to achieve
humiliation glory vacancies
but you don't want your firearms preconceived-
they are moments of defiant history.
The dream begins with stunning poverty.
One never gets the thanks deserved, and he
was working for a controversial fee
and structural adjustment novel pleas
written as a fast-paced thriller. Read
the gripping book. The captain of the team
fulfills your tart objectives in degrees,
certificates, credential referees.
Horizontal competition leagues
regenerating Super Bowl fatigue.

My face from Middle English, not designed
to replace the language places, human rights,
and mathematics prism arts comply
with Incident Command or training flights.
Aggressive styling seized large swathes of coarse
performance, facts are sacred truth-
fundamental, hopeless, downbeat source.
They actually went and did it! Finished smooth.
The mantis shrimp, a favorite breaking up
distilling voice from rumor in despair,
but science learning English from behind
the boring headline drones exploring prayer,
extremists counter late atomic clocks
pulling stupid punches over stocks.

Intended to belong to medicine
in connection with equipment needs,
the army closet dishes Klonopin-
not as useless as the truth can be.
You'd want to end the loop under control
of optional expression articles.
This may promote a quality of soul
conditional break statement miracles
instead of executed language truth
cognate with Frisian structure quality
preventing guidelines, semicolon truth
forever followed integral disease,
adaptive sports where everyone can play
a decent place for campaigns of decay.

Having training to perform a task
with knowledge and experience required
machinist rehab lifestyle choices fast,
filling holes in native labor spires,
expressive entry searches sponsored fonts
You must nominate an occupation list
from independent family, relevant
philosophies of allocations missed.
Successful migrant visas greenlight care
recruiting foreign workers' industry
with chemical migration wear and tear
assisted living seeking nominees.
It's helping people get the joint they need
to find a job improving Japanese.

Encyclopedic satisfaction lies

misleading, flat-out joint replacement terms,

exaggerated striking nationwide

and academic studies reaffirm

decisions proven complex overviews

and fluent research universities

intended for professionals experts choose

veterinary country treatment fees

related to the therapeutic hold

while scientific ethics journals sink

the free press dietetics, uncontrolled

San Francisco doctors interlink

prescription stone extractor lines afloat

while launching aircraft carriers by remote.

but sometimes after navigating sheer
location routing, mapping enterprise
intelligence, a special atmosphere-
the oceanic grammar will surprise
the clock which shows the alcoholic plants,
the marketplace security exchange,
the drinking club, a pagan cult of chants-
progressive populations fire downrange
for private execution galleries
attacking ransom overwhelmed by fear,
held hostage over telescopic keys
to formal ties with British mutineers
confusing explanations- they will find
a time machine to travel back and pine.

Related species patterns over time,
environmental economic fields
acceptably consistent with the prime
directive factor stimuli they wield.
The influential neural pathway acts
responding to external action states-
strategic concepts backing up the fact
of operant conditioning tempting fate.
Disordered populations who control
dementia's progress and resilient hope
get insight into their caregiver's roles
while dealing with audacity of "nope."
Genetic fluctuations will prepare
Adventist corporations in midair.

Let's be clear: the family killed my father
with needless systematic bill of rights
of passage struggling, diagnostic slaughter,
and rising well-intentioned bad advice.
We'd like to know your thoughts around the world.
Get a free no-obligation quote
enabling Catholic bishops' flags unfurled-
it looks as if compounded prospects float
millions after tax alignment laws
overwhelmed by complicated sets.
Revolution's triage worldwide caused
diversified affairs of governments,
vocabularies otherwise not known
to bureaucrats left hanging on the phone.

Proposal obligations 'round the world,
superlative asylum classic sports-
neurotic ethics standard gizmo pearl
given as a rule instead of quartz.
Superlative freelancer refugees
with vastly different independent thoughts
ensure that comics dither magazine
improvement and remodeling zoning lots
for the public prison access libel source
protecting Lockheed Martin engineers
from discipline of space-time vector force
and diabetics wet behind the ears.
Learn how it works and launch a civil war-
explosive confrontations we ignore.

Expressing meaning moving toward a point
approaching dumb ways oscillating place.
Dying contents indicate the joint
untrammeled destinations just in case
broader dollar softness impacts trade.
Don't forget to close all cookie jars,
browser windows, log out when you're done.
NASA says don't worry about guitars.
Fidelity distractions leading us to ruin
reverse the damaged asteroid fly-by.
Send money, pay online- the bedouin
Rosetta's on a slow connection high.
In love with anyone? You'll love dumb pipes
that play your favorite music stars and stripes.

The present gerund participle bears
all the weight of voluntary leave-
a hundred columns reinforcing airs
underpinning girders misconceived
by hundred column champions shored up roles
sustaining lost capacity of life
and grieving daughters' independent souls
enduring solace-giving leading strife.
Struggles undermine their pass defense
subordinate to the leading parts of speech.
Contradict the argument pretense
secondary cornerbacks in reach.
Substructure consolation drivers work
assistance convoys need distressed benchmarks.

To harness power, light to energy
from artificial sources recognized
under custom law of lethargy
a state bestowing duties emphasized
sentries, traders advocating greed
for a healthy world by making saints.
Join the triumph celebrating need
united by disastrous free complaints
with rigorous rebellion breaking out
evacuating information breach
with wine and cheese convenience bringing doubt
to comfortable subsidiary speech-
independent declarations run
designated with an asterisk undone.

Belonging governed by a mental state
persuaded by the cancer in New York
from Indo-European language gates
abbreviated overtime for torque
translation moments, carbon dating sites-
the stressed descendant photographs and needs,
tuberculosis credit cards and plights
resulting from a death, the lungs concede
vibration cornerstones were underlaid
specializing ethnically diverse
jet propulsion guzzling lemonade
across the country teaching unrhymed verse-
pentrametry an outlawed pagan cult
corrupting modern children and adults.

Lymphoblastic chocolate thinking bass
acknowledge recipes and confidence-
desserts and onion chicken just in case
hell has broken loose. Progressive sense
detergent stain removal reconciled
ourselves with God for fascinating art,
spectacular particular lifestyles
taken collectively to tear apart
climate change, the green economy,
growing Mississippi children's lives
with parenthood destroying families-
a low point for the hope they will survive.
That doesn't mean alluring ladies care,
it only shows the spacecraft wasn't there.

Glycation product worsening of time,
geologic epoch smaller parts-
successive strata laid down overnight,
a single geologic pile of charts
existed when a person becomes blue
diversionary tactics Cleveland likes.
Take a look and see what they can do.
This comic drinking images for spiked
intelligence and conversation melt
unattested Vulgar Latin songs.
Britannica interpreted fan belts
driving sonic romance all along.
Bundesministerium hat die
mit einer in Zusammenhang aktie.

Moreover: human centers for disease
control, prevention, cyanide tonight
favor happy grammar guarantees
navigating habitats of blight,
friendly Scandinavian great concerns,
Nordic immigration management,
restless preservation of returns
in a mini-dress with high heel sacraments-
my go-to combination circuit lies
in engineering context of the text
protection science journals prize-
Cheech and Chong progressive intersex,
aficionado recreation guides
to integrative science suicides.

Possessive rights as citizens of Rome
used afterlife convenience, probably
full of problems like the ones at home
presented by most native English speak,
pronounced the way advancing cultures read.
Contraction workers shouldn't wash their hands.
Irregardless, princesses buzz feed-
it doesn't last forever. Understand
those guys who burned that man alive ignore
the captivating unique violent strength,
the full potential inauthentic selves
vaccinating children drain at length.
The real reason women freeze their eggs
is open-ended value exercise.

Parents and their children, as a group
a taxonomic order victims lose
grounded on the principal blood loop-
unselfish, honest, loyal overuse.
It took a hundred years to build the thing
and just a few decisions of life's work
to lose the scrapbook's other helpful hints-
uncountable, immediate, gone berzerk.
The Church of Jesus Christ, who lost control
of center city Philadelphia
after thirteen years of war, extol
the benefits of word dyslexia
through spare, appealing color photographs.
I didn't find the battles worth the laughs.

Accompanied direction form of light

changes in a systematic way

possessing something flower-sprigged and white

in opposition, fighting angry play.

Leave it trembling- I will go for you.

He fought his brother, enemy in place

together reimagining the hew

becoming clear why slingshot poker face

flagship murder measures modern love

playing strings, banana peels, and good

spacesuits matching airline boxing gloves.

A one-night stand exchanging hybrid wood

realizes when those things go south

you're likely to get pasted in the mouth.

Horrendous killing partnership with faith,

cartoon truth, and abstract battle plans-

a treadmill change. Pope Francis compact wraiths

said "Don't believe in everything." You can

appreciate crap beer dysfunction more,

but rarely do those problems reach some hill

neutrality administration's door.

Geographic lion cubs distill

South Africa's reserve alliance drive-

conservancy songwriters, spotlight fame,

rattlesnakes and wedding rings alive,

and rescue missions broadcasting acclaim

creating, sharing, celebrating childhood-

mysterious rebels of walking dead make good.

Hordes of tourists, piles of rubble form

courtroom drama common freakout snubs,

burdened cricket moment funny farms,

and billboard update generation hubs.

The deprivation knowledge of the flesh–

the spring of 1984, I went

to free-throw lines defying Arctic stench

across a hundred sacrifices of vets

ensuring that their legacies are banned.

Common factor microimagery

determined engineering questions planned

weakness empires, inexplicably

reviled scintillating Breath of God.

Dirty Karma Service gets the nod.

Circumstances turn and break New York,
a tribulation image suffers fear-
worrying flash of light toward the sky.
And I am not afraid of what you hear-
a thousand eyes, eleventh day of change
around the world: uncertain culture risk
exposure- hijacked in four planes,
commitment resource unable to fix
trajectories of unrelenting war
accelerating troubling global space
rebuilding cities stronger than they were
divided, independent hiding place.
Designated areas in the zone
devastated complex towers blown.

Intended useless parenthetic truth
separated terminated need
increment expressions with vermouth,
forever dictionaries faced by teens:
adaptive sports and Cleveland dealers teach
our future on their shoulders' fellowship
beginning student violence impeached
your confident performance with pink slips.
Silicone ideas searching sex
criteria granting changes underground
meditation licensing complex
matchups, think tank justice runaround.
Future efforts' fresh new look and feel
exploited children missing sprocket wheels.

ACKNOWLEDGEMENTS

First, I owe a debt of gratitude to Bernadette Mayer, whose off-the-cuff joke about the sonnet form during a webcast at the Kelly Writers House formed the nucleus around which this book was built.

Thanks as always to Kenneth Goldsmith, for his championing of conceptual, uncreative writing as well as for his kind support in the writing of my first two books.

I remain especially grateful for the friendship, mentorship, and encouragement of Al Filreis. As you already know, you taught me what I know of writing and poetry, and it was you who introduced me to Bernadette Mayer's work and who hosted her at KWH when she made her wonderful sonnet joke. It's an absolute privilege to be your CTA, and I could never thank you enough for all you've given me.

I would also like to thank Al and Mandana Chaffa, Therese Pope, Karren Aleiner, Nicola Quinn, T. de los Reyes, and Mark Herron for their encouragement and friendship, and for reviewing these sonnets while the work was in progress.

Thank you to my daughters Hayley and Melanie, who inspire me to be the best father I can be, and who lovingly forgive my shortcomings.

I am very grateful to my wife Pamela. Your love and encouragement remains essential to me, and I couldn't do this without you. Thanks for not freaking out when I said I was gonna quit my job.

Mark Snyder grew up in Evergreen Park, Illinois. He serves as a Community TA in the course in Modern and Contemporary American Poetry at Coursera.org under Prof. Al Filreis. He has written three other experimental works: *Epitaph, Come As You Are, and Vatadu,* and created two albums of experimental music- *Necessary Evil* and *Requiem-* the latter a secular conceptual setting of the Mass composed in the days immediately prior to the death of his father. He lives in rural North Carolina and practices psychiatry at a state psychiatric hospital. He lives with his wife and daughters.

www.ingramcontent.com/pod-product-compliance
Lightning Source LLC
Chambersburg PA
CBHW060717030426
42337CB00017B/2899